OGUGUA-GEE O

Keep Doing What Really Matters

Motivational Messages for Teachers

What teachers tell us

" Ogugua Okolo-Angus has a huge rich bundle of knowledge and insightfully knows how to motivate and inspire teachers. She provides much hope to all teachers and senior leaders in our schools."

Joan Deslandes OBE, Headteacher, Kingsford Community School, London.

"Ogugua is supportive in her work with headteachers and senior leadership teams. She always gives more of her time and energy to school leaders in order to improve the way they see themselves."

Neil Harvey, Ex Headteacher, Oasis Academy and Lead Ofsted Inspector.

"Ogugua exudes a 'can do' attitude which has been very refreshing and assists the school leaders and teachers greatly in specific areas of need."

Louise Robertson, Allen Edwards Primary School, London.

"Ogugua's support is invaluable. She is an exceptionally astute and perceptive leader and educator willing and able to both support with precision and insight."

Adam Twyman, Headteacher, Holy Trinity Lamorbey (Part of Amadeus Academy Primary Trust)

For information regarding coaching, conferences, workshops, seminars, and training sessions (virtual or face-to-face), please make contact using the information below:

Dr Ogugua-Gee Okolo- Angus (Founder and Education Director of Change Agents in Action)

www.changeagentsinaction.co.uk/

admin@changeagentsinaction.co.uk

Instagram: changeagents_action

Facebook: Change Agents in Action Ltd

LinkedIn: changeagentsin action

Designed by Ogugua-Gee Okolo-Angus using canva.com

ISBN: 978-1-5272-9431-8

Dedication

Keep Doing What Really Matters is dedicated to all those who are working through their 'own stuff' in order to be a positive presence in the lives of others. It is an appreciation of the inner work you are doing so that you can show up as the very best example of yourself.

Acknowledgements

With the deepest gratitude, I want to thank every person who has come into my life and touched it in some way. I acknowledge all of my 'teachers' who continue to shape my life experiences. The many lessons I continue to learn encourages me to fulfil my life work.

I acknowledge both my late mother and late father in providing the many life lessons that have made me resilient and kept me focused. Their foresight, intuition and courage have afforded me the tenacious spirit I have today. My mother and father inspired me to strive through struggle and to continuously push past pain. I use their far-sightedness to rise above challenges that I face in my life.

My son who is my most precious gift alongside my soulmate inspires me each and every day; continuously providing purpose and meaning in my life.

Above all things, I am spiritually guided and that has uplifted me, kept me going throughout this journey; for which I give all thanks.

Where I have referenced the quotations in this book, there is an acknowledgement of thoughts and original ideas from others. I profusely apologise if I have quoted without proper citation, misquoted, or unknowingly altered the quotation of anyone.

About the Author

By my nature and disposition, I am a self-motivated transformational educationalist. I live and work through my moral lens and continue to be optimistic about helping to create ' a world-class' education system that is limitless, boundless, and 'easily' accessible to all students and young people regardless of race, class, gender, age, ability, advantage, or disadvantage. Despite setbacks I continue to see challenges in education as simply obstacles to get over. This is because I am infectiously enthusiastic about school leadership and the development of others. I turn my enthusiasm, interest, and social consciousness into helping to build world class schools; locating myself in such a way as to develop practical solutions that can be easily implemented, embedded, and sustained. I am an advocate of reform where it is necessary. I am principled, very principled about social justice, equity, equality of opportunity and fairness in schools.

I have come to learn more about myself as a result of my daily reflections and believe that the purpose of my life work is to uplift, support, encourage but also challenge (with love!) educators in their pursuit of excellence for all the children and young people they serve. In building my knowledge through observations of the world and social interactions, I have written this book as a reference point for you to stand in your own consciousness and reflect on the impact you have in the world today.

If you are '*any type*' of teacher anywhere in the world, this book is for you. To me, a teacher is anyone dedicated to enlightening, motivating and inspiring others. A teacher is anyone who tirelessly does for others and gives something of themselves in the process. A teacher is anyone who cares enough to make a positive difference in the lives of others. And in that context, I attest that at some point in our lives we all are teachers! This book serves to enlighten, encourage, and engage you to consider the importance of introspection and reflection. This is so that your awareness of **Keep Doing What Really Matters** is the guiding principle for the impact you have on the people who show up in your life and look to you to do good for them in their lives.

Introduction

I was born at the height of the Biafran war; a civil war in West Africa that ravaged a nation and senselessly slaughtered babies and young children in 1967. Although not located there, my parents felt a strong sense of connection to their roots, culture and their home and saw the importance of maintaining ties with our family 'back home'. They ensured that I along with my siblings had secure knowledge of our rich history. At the time of the Biafran war, I entered into this world and my parents named me Ogugua. For them, at the time of unrest, unease, and devastation it was important to give me a name that means comfort, purpose, and service. When I was about 8 years old, I vaguely remember them telling me that they had given me this Igbo name as they believed I would live up its meaning and responsibility. They imagined that I would serve children whose voices were lost or diminished, and as if they could see into the future, they were right. It is with that upbringing that I came to learn the significance and importance of my name. I realised much later when I was a teenager that being given the name Ogugua was actually my calling. It was a name that would determine my footsteps through life and would propel me into life work for making a positive difference to children and young people. I talk often of my late mother and late father's foresight and in so doing over the years have come to appreciate myself as a teacher, educator and servant who seeks to inspire others to be the very best example of themselves.

Keep Doing What Really Matters is intended to be a mirror for *all sorts of teachers* to look into each day as a way for self-honouring ourselves, finding inner strength and engaging in reflective practice. This is so that we give to others the very best of ourselves because we care about how we show up in the world. This book serves to support those teachers who at moments in their life need support to recognise, acknowledge and accept their strengths and areas they are working on.

In this book, I hope to impart some lessons that enable *all teachers* to see themselves as Change Agents in Action who seek to respond to the needs in education where it really matters. This is so that children and young people especially those ***who are disadvantaged by the education they receive*** may shine like the stars they were always meant to be.

Whilst reading this book you might want to consider all that you continue to do as a teacher who inspires and uplifts others. Specifically, you might want to acknowledge your commitment to social justice, education reform and the betterment of all school systems that decrees meaningful success for all children and young people.

In this book you will find that I talk much about conscious thoughts, conscious habits, and conscious decisions. This is because I realise that in taking decisive steps for making a difference to the lives of children and young people, I believe that we must be guided by a purposefully planned approach to the actions we take. Some of the points made throughout this book recur periodically and this is how it is intended. It is to emphasise essential aspects of our work as educators that we must always be conscious of and reflect upon.

I have used quotes from various people to emphasis the points I am making in each section of the book in order to frame the lessons I am suggesting we can learn. This book is really about introspection so that what we tell ourselves projects into the world through our personal conviction as we advocate for equity and social justice in schools.

To be a child or young person at this time can be challenging especially if born into any form of disadvantage. This is not to complain or protest but to recognise the obstacles that can hinder children and young people's progress through life. For centuries, schools have always been defined by their vision, mission, and values. However, for some, the experience that children and young people receive can render them hostage to a life of suffering and limitations. And so, having teachers to uplift their spirits can often be the best tonic for their souls.

This book extends the hope that through self-analysis and self-examination, as educators we may serve to change the education landscape by being consciously present in our own mission and purpose. And in so doing we may truly embody a commitment to assist our children in the best way we know. This is so that we can be sure to radiate positive messages that make a demonstrable difference in the lives of children and young people who need us most.

Everything

''Everything from here on

is important

Every way we do things

is important

What we all say about the education of children and young people

is important

How we support, encourage, and motivate children and young people

is important

The way we seek to eradicate injustices

is important

What we say to each other about the children and young people whom the education system disadvantages

is important

The society that we are helping to rebuild and reimagine

is important

What children and young people think, feel, and say about themselves

is important

How we work together to change the narrative in our education system

is important

If we realise this, then for all the efforts we make, our greatest successes are in each child we teach and reach!''

Ogugua-Gee Okolo-Angus

Conscious Thoughts

Self-Discovery

One day, it all clicks and makes perfect sense

Unknown

I trust that you will see your worth. I hope that in this very moment you will realise just how important you are. I wish for you to know how far you have come and all that you have achieved. I hope you know that the battles you have fought to get here and the struggles you have endured have led you to your rightful place. I wish for you to connect with your soul in that you experience a sense of fulfilment for your life work. It is my hope that have reached a point in your life in which you realise your worth and significance. I trust that your higher level of consciousness is helping you see your greatness. It is my desire for you to discover the wonderful self within so that you connect with your greatest being. I hope that you have discovered your passion for teaching, for learning and for healing. In spending time with your authentic self, I hope that you hold your passion and purpose close, accepting the natural vibrations of your greatness.

One day it all makes sense, and I trust that today is the day.

Conscious Thought

Helping others

Helping others is the way to help ourselves

Oprah Winfrey

This is what I have learnt:

- When you do good, good always follows
- There is nothing more satisfying than knowing you played a small yet significant part in making someone smile
- Being of service is a special kind of blessing
- Helping others to reach for their goals is an intrinsic reward in itself
- Giving unconditionally is one of the truest and purest blessings
- Your small acts of kindness can be the beacon of hope and light to others
- Inspiring others to be the best version of themselves uplifts all humankind
- Giving meaning in other people's lives provides a satisfying feeling for the difference you make
- The goodness you pour into other people's lives supports their growth
- Lightening the burden for others serves as a pathway to end their suffering and pain

This is my time to do good for others without expectation.

Integrity

Choosing courage over comfort; choosing what is right over what is fun, fast, or easy and choosing to practise our values rather than simply professing them

Brene Brown

I tell myself the truth about myself and commit to my moral obligation which is the virtue that completes me. I am always guided by my moral compass and principally maintain the highest of standards that I determine. My character is fuelled with conscious thoughts that direct my footsteps and order my conscious actions. I do the right thing because it is the right thing to be done. I choose courage over comfort and practice this value daily. I live as a demonstration of the role model I have always intended to be. My integrity to do what is right even when it goes unnoticed is the fundamental value of truth I uphold. In fairness and in truth I always do what is right even if at times it is not easy.

In fairness and in truth for the good of myself and others I remain honourable, principled, and fair. That is my moral code, and I am sticking to it!

Uncompromising values

Be a leader who will take an uncompromising stand to establish truth

Sunday Adelaja

I refuse to accept anything less than what is just and of value. I continue to be the opponent of injustice and inequality. I continue my unwavering commitment to excellence no matter what is happening around me. I am the truth, speak the truth and live the truth in all circumstances. I do not excuse anyone for the suffering they cause to children. Where there is disadvantage, I serve to eradicate it in the most productive way possible. I always hold true to my values, especially when it comes to children born into disadvantage. My mission to provide a quality first learning experience will always continue no matter the challenges I may encounter. I am deeply rooted in my belief that children's lives matter. I stand uncompromisingly in my space, deep-rooted in fairness, equity, social change, and equality.

Today is the day that I as a teacher take an uncompromising step towards realising that I am within my right to do what is absolutely necessary for the good of all children.

Gratitude

The more thankful I became, the more my bounty increased. That's because for sure – what you focus on expands. When you focus on the goodness in life, you create more of it

Oprah Winfrey

I am grateful for all that I am, and all that I have experienced. I am grateful for the blessings that have been bestowed upon me, even when at times I did not see them as such. I am grateful for the trials and tribulations that have made me stronger. I am grateful for the rich and varied experiences of my life that have given me a sense of purpose. I am grateful for the goodness that pours into my life bringing calmness, quiet and peace. I am grateful for the magnet of miracles that I have attracted into my life that have shielded me from negativity and pain. I am grateful for the inspirational people who surround me, providing life lessons that I may learn from. I am grateful for the hurt that I have encountered, for it has increased my awareness of my strength. I am grateful for the rejections I have received because they have given me the opportunity to propel myself forward with purpose. And in so choosing to be grateful each day, I experience more positive things that sooth my soul and comfort my heart. As an antidote to negativity, I choose to be grateful for all my lessons. For I know and believe that no matter how bad things seem there is always some aspect of my life for which I can be thankful. Being grateful makes me know that just as I am, I can do all things because just as I am is enough.

I shall rejoice in the splendour of gratitude for it is the mediation for my heart and mind that is incredibly good for my soul.

Wisdom

The man who views the world at fifty the same way he did at twenty has wasted thirty years of his life

Muhammad Ali

You have a profound impact on the lives of many children and young people in your care. With such a responsibility it seems wise to understand your life lessons. Even if they seem insignificant, they will enable you to believe that there is nothing that is outside of you more powerful than what is inside of you. Wisdom allows you to follow your heart whilst consciously using matters of your mind for determining your next steps. It allows you to embark upon a life journey in which to build the very best version of yourself having learnt from your experiences. It will sustain you in your bleakest of hours and will guide you to the path of contentment so that even in the chaos of life will you be able to appreciate your greatness.

Be patient with yourself and know that all that you are seeking to achieve will manifest in the goodness of time. Choose to organise your life such that there is only space for positive vibrations. Remain in this space through all the walks of your life and see your experiences manifest in the most positive of ways. For it is at those times when you will be filled with enthusiasm, optimism, and hope.

I am creating a positive life for myself and using my wisdom in all circumstances.

Willingness

My success is measured by my willingness to keep trying

Anonymous

When we decide to act for the good of others, we open our minds to continually developing and enhancing our teaching skills. We know that at times we have to be willing to look at our flaws as an empowering process for improvement. This is the guiding route that enables us to willingly do better for the children whom we serve. And even in the most turbulent of times when we do what is unfamiliar, we acknowledge this in order to change ourselves. We become willing to accept all that we are and all that we portray in the world. We affirm this in order to change our habits as well as our thoughts when this is necessary. We do this with a conscious heart because we know we have children's lives in our hands, and we must be willing to do all that we can to ensure their success.

I commit to hearing my inner voice that tells me the importance of looking at my shortcomings as an empowering way to change myself for the better.

Energy

Energy is neither created nor destroyed

Julius Robert Mayer

What type of energy do I hold in my heart? What do I emit from this energy? How does this energy show up when I am doing my work as an educator? If energy can never be destroyed, what am I holding onto and is it good for my soul? Am I surrounding myself with positive energy? How is the energy that radiates from my spirit showing up in other people's lives? What type of energy am I renewing and reusing? Am I aware that my energy is everything and may be contagious? What are the ways for maintaining positive energy regardless of any life experiences? Is the energy I am consuming good for my mind, body, and soul? How are my energy frequencies keeping me grounded and alert to what my body is telling me? Does my energy make someone smile today? Does my energy make someone shine today? Does my energy create success in others? Does my energy flow positively to all those who need it?

I commit to using my positive energy to make a significant difference to the lives of children who need it most.

Perception

If you want to achieve greatness stop asking for permission

Unknown

People do what they do based on their perceptions of reality. Reality is a socially constructed process shaped by our experiences and ideals. When we know who we are and do not question it, we obtain the answers from within. We see things not as they are but as we are and that is what makes our perceptions real. We have to understand how we must perceive our life to be able to determine the decisions we must make. The decisions we make can lead us to a perspective in life that enlightens our minds and brings us joy. Our perception can be easy or hard depending on how we shift our thinking. What we choose to believe actually makes us who we are. So, in all things, we can intuitively let our positive perceptions of ourselves create the blossoms in our lives, making it more fruitful.

The nature of my perceptions means that I can create positive realities for my life.

Personal Effectiveness

I prefer to be true to myself, even at the hazard of incurring the ridicule of others

Frederick Douglass

Notes to self:

I am a learner who improves with experience

I have self-drive and am motivated to always do my best

I create opportunities for myself and keep growing and learning more

I have positive learning habits that create success

I internalise my personal victories because they strengthen me

I visualise all that I want for myself so that I can realise my talents

I have developed positive images of myself so that they show up like that in the world

I realise the precious gifts I hold within me, for me and by me

I recognise the steps I need to continue to take so I can do my life work with conviction

I acknowledge the channels for ensuring a positive mindset

I accept all that I am, all that I have and all that I can do

Today I shall remind myself of my talents and gifts that make me who I have decided to become.

Dreams

The future belongs to those who believe in the beauty of their dreams

Eleanor Roosevelt

I sit in my empty classroom and I dream big. I create re-imagined possibilities for a world in which there is balance, harmony, and peace. I keep trusting in my dreams believing them to be the start of making a difference for the children in my care. I re-create opportunities in which all human beings are recognised for the positive contributions they make in this world. To keep my dreams alive, I hold onto my belief that makes all things seem possible. And with this, I re-develop the learning environment in which educators give everything they have to uplift all children in their care. This is because educators dare to do better. They dare to change the narrative in their pursuit of excellence. They dare to remain colour blind. Educators open their hearts and minds to unconscious undertakings that guide their moral purpose. They promise never to give up on any child who arrives in their classroom. Educators believe they can, and so they do.

Today I choose to dream big and follow my dreams to my highest personal conviction so that I may continue to do good for others.

Proud

We see all that you are and all that you do

Ogugua-Gee Okolo-Angus

You are doing the best you can; believe this does not go unnoticed. Believe in the progress that your students are making. Believe in the way you have helped others so selflessly just because you care. Believe in how you show up every day and give your students your best. Believe in the tough decisions you make and stand your ground for the good of your students. Believe in your far-sightedness whilst using past experiences as part of your growth and learning. Believe in the way you see endless possibilities for the children you hold in your heart. Their goals have been reached because you set your intentions rightly. Your relentless focus on excellence makes all things seem worthwhile. Believe your students are proud because you give them a fighting chance to thrive. Believe they salute you because you fight ignorance and do all you can to eliminate inequality. Believe your students are humbled by all that you continue to do.

We see you; we hear you; we know you; and we are proud of you.

Success

I am gonna show you how great I am

Muhammad Ali

Not by accident but by design you graduated from your class in your teaching institution. Not by accident but by design you have been given the important role for determining a child's pathway. Your deepest passion for success for all children has made your teaching more powerful. All that you have been doing since your training has enabled you to teach with personal conviction. The service you give to others has created their success. You hold their achievements as if they were your own because you crave every opportunity for them to shine. You may think you are ordinary, but you most certainly create extraordinary learning experiences. You know your critics well and that only helps you to see things rightly. Giving up on the children in your care has never been an option. You put no limits on what you can achieve, nor do for the success of others. It is all this and more that makes you the great human instrument of hope and inspiration.

You show the world just how great you are through the successful opportunities you have created for others.

Conscious Thought

Uniqueness

Life is like wearing your uniqueness like your identity badge

Anonymous

Teaching is the opportunity for you to:

- Be noticed for your gifts and talents
- Be your authentic self
- Embrace your greatness and the way you do things
- Stay in your own lane in pursuit of excellence
- Accept your true individual gifts and talents
- Celebrate yourself as the cornerstone of courage
- Become who you determine is important
- Shine like the star you are
- Make a difference in your own divine way
- Use your power responsively

Today I commit to my own self-expression as a reflection of my uniqueness.

Unity

Our ability to reach unity in diversity will be the beauty and test of our civilisation

Mahatma Gandhi

Thank you for creating the climate in which your students can collaborate not compete. Thank you for recognising the strength of building together so that every child can succeed. You do all that you can to ensure a collaborative classroom culture that advocates for unity. You know that you cannot force people to work together. You cannot force them to recognise the power in collaboration. But by enabling the children to lean on each other you get them to appreciate each other's strengths. This is unity in its purest sense because you shout out to the world that diversity can and must be celebrated. You provide the vital tools for this to happen as you design your learning environment. This lets us all know that diversity is a gift as we become connected through our differences.

Thank you for showing us that in unity there is magnificence and strength.

Conscious Thought

Mission

I am on my personal mission to give the very best of myself

Ogugua-Gee Okolo-Angus

What is your mission?

Some teachers say to:

- Have an absolute devotion to my goals
- Take risks that others may feel is too dangerous
- Come out of my comfort zone
- Continue to be filled with enthusiasm
- Continue to be filled with optimism
- Integrate my mission with my vision
- Hold true to my values
- Provide the direction I need to succeed
- Always teach with integrity
- Make a significant difference in the lives of those who need me most

I commit to my mission that determines how I will work for others.

Self-Awareness

Awareness is the greatest agent for change

Eckhart Tolle

The more I learn about myself, the more I realise that:

- ✓ There is wisdom in my teaching because I build upon my experiences
- ✓ I have a clear identity because of what I stand for and believe in
- ✓ My reputation precedes me, and I am known for the good I do in this world
- ✓ I am developing my teaching brand of care and consideration for all young people
- ✓ My honest self-reflections are part of my authentic mirror talk that holds me accountable
- ✓ I am clear about the positive contributions I make
- ✓ The perception of how I show up in my classroom is accepted from my students because of my determination to always want to be my best
- ✓ My internal awareness is enabling me to recognise the power of my teaching
- ✓ My objective evaluations of my teaching help the next learning experience to be better

As a change agent I use self-awareness and reflection to improve my teaching practice.

Willpower

Strength comes from indomitable will

Mahatma Gandhi

Teacher voices:

I will move mountains so that children get the best education they deserve

I will create opportunities for my students to be successful

I will challenge all stereotypes that limit the progress of my students

I will change the narrative by being responsive to need

I will commit to the pursuit of excellence

I will strive to do good no matter what

I will make decisions that empowers others

I will dedicate myself to ensuring the achievement of children who I serve

I will see the impossible as possible

I will keep motivating myself to do better

I will use the power of my mind to determine the people I need to reach.

Change Agents make a difference

The first step to getting somewhere is to decide you are not going to remain where you are

Unknown

Never doubt the difference you make in this world. Never apologise for the decisions you take when using your voice where it is most needed. Remember the changes you make even if it just in one person's world. Remember to focus on what you may have to sacrifice if only to accomplish what is necessary.

You are the flower that blossoms in the midst of the thorns. You transform the world around you. You are that dependable constant that keeps on developing because you keep believing. You are leading a new beginning and doing it so purposefully. You are the transformational change because you make the change happen.

I am the change agent that makes a difference in my own significant way!

Conscious Thought

Change Agents make Conscious Choices

You get what you tolerate

Unknown

A teacher once said:

I am too formidable to let others diminish my worth. The good I see within me is what I will continue to project out into the world. I am not afraid to shine because there are sun rays within me. I listen to my heart and the decisions I take are the right ones because I feel their purpose. I have developed a level of consciousness that motivates me to do more. The wisdom I have supports me in protecting my emotional wealth. My conscious choices put no limitation on what is possible. My conscious thoughts leave an impression in my mind and are always positive. I live with purpose. I work with purpose and I consciously commit to it!

My conscious mind only has space for positive thoughts!

Virtuous

Virtue lies within our power

Aristotle

Nothing beats virtue! And as the cornerstone of our lives, we interrupt the patterns of negativity, spreading much joy along the way. This brings with it a heartfelt desire in wanting to help others. There is no pretence in our actions because we reflect all that is good. Our character is noble as we are the definition of dignity and grace. We gain the strength we need for holding onto our values. And in this way, we practice simple virtuous living. Our kindness creates sunshine in other people's hearts because there is goodness in our souls.

We simply deal with matters of the heart and live through it with purpose!

Self-Awareness

Self-Awareness involves deep personal honesty

Stephen Covey

This is who I am:

I am honest because I tell the truth

I focus on integrity because my moral compass guides me

I make life-changing decisions because I am courageous

I do not judge myself but look for lessons in all my experiences

I am fearless, especially when it is about equity and fairness

I perceptively diminish all forms of negativity when I experience it

I pay attention to my thoughts and words as they determine my actions and disposition

I remain mindful in all situations so that I can respond appropriately

I am brave in the pursuit of excellence

I dare to challenge the stereotype because it is important for me to do so

I know my strengths and I use them positively.

Courage

Courage is grace under pressure

Ernest Hemingway

We must put faith in our ability to change things that we consider to be wrong. It calls for us to put aside anything that causes us to fear and recognise that courage will instil in us a sense of purpose. Courage enables us to make a stand in order to strive through our toughest battles. Courage can often be the quiet voice that remains rooted in possibility or the loud trumpet blowing fanfare that so boldly calls for action. Whichever the path, courage taken is that brave moment of truth that allows us to be known for the values we hold. And in this way, it sets the tone for living and working with integrity for the children and young people whom we care about. Our courage defines our character especially when we see things going wrong.

We hold onto our memories of bravery and courage, knowing that it is enabling us to make the changes we need to see in this uneven world!

Purpose

I know why the caged bird sings!

Paul Laurence Dunbar

Are there times when you question why you do what you do? Have you thought about the reasons you stay where you are despite the challenges? At times you may reflect on your current position as an educator and feel constrained because of the external factors weighing you down. Maybe you feel the pressures of having to conform or perhaps you are just so tired of all that the education system has done to you. This might show up as frustration, anger, guilt and even suffering. But despite the caged feeling you may experience, you still have the ability to show up, doing your best and giving your best. Perhaps it is your passion that is creating the climate for teaching with purpose. Maybe it is believing that your life work as a teacher has the desire to have a tremendous impact in this world. It might be that it provides the very reason for inspiring hope in the minds of children who look up to you knowing that you will do well by them. Whatever the reason, your sense of purpose is the starting point for healing all ills no matter the challenge!

Today, I make my decision for ensuring that I am working through my purpose with passion!

Optimism

I didn't care what happened, the glass was always going to be half full.

Quincy Jones

I can, I will, I shall, I am able to, it is possible, it is necessary, it can be done, it will be done! Just one such mantra to hold in your heart when the going gets tough. If all seems bleak, remember times when you tried and prevailed. Think back to an experience when you overcame the challenges and saw them as obstacles to jump over. Consciously develop a conditioned response to any form of adversity. It will support you being kind to yourself. Prevail in your own way, as hope for a future generation that needs your encouragement and inspiration. This is your claim to a future filled with possibilities. Your positive thinking is your self-styled moral courage. As you adapt yourself to every situation, you enthusiastically embrace changes in your circumstances with eyes, souls, and minds wide open.

I will always seek to be enthusiastic, to remain optimistic and feed my mind with positive thoughts so that I can be at my best.

Resilience

In order to make dreams come into reality, it takes an awful lot of determination, dedication, self-discipline, and effort.
Jesse Owens

Resilience confirms your tenacious spirit. It defines all that you are as a person of courage. It enables you to hang onto hope and to bear any suffering for the greater good. It envelopes your life work as an educator because it creates the capacity of you to maintain your core purpose despite the challenges. During tough times, resilience defines who you want to become. It might lead you to a new reality which can amount to new strength and more powerful thoughts. So never give up even in the face of adversity. Just know that as part of your human experience, your hard-won battles will cultivate meaningful, optimistic, and purposeful experiences in your life.

I will keep going no matter what. For I truly believe that when the going gets tough, the strongest, bravest soldiers show up and keep focused and determined.

Strength

The struggle you are in today is developing the strength you need tomorrow

Anonymous

You are your greatest hero. Affirm this each and every day. In moments of weakness and despair, gain strength by understanding that your toughest times are battles you will overcome. Use your mirror reflections to look for all signs of inner strength. Look deeply into your eyes and notice that your gaze is affirming you as a true warrior. The expressions on your face are the reflections of all that you have been through and survived. Listen intently to your breath, for as you inhale you take with it the courage to keep going even when all things appear daunting. Pushing yourself and battling against the odds supports your belief that you will conquer your most challenging experiences. And even in the face of adversity, your strength will enable you to carry yourself through the storms comforting your soul as you travel. And as you surround yourself with this strength, remember to recognise, acknowledge, and accept your power. For it is this strength that will carry you to the end of the rainbow, creating your own sunshine, even in the midst of darkness.

I am strong because I have weathered storms. I am strong because I have expanded my courage and now, I believe I am unbeaten and unbroken!

Foresight

Have a vision. Be demanding
Colin Powell

A distinctive aspect of foresight is anticipating the future and preparing for it. But at the same time, it is using hindsight as a learning process for doing better next time around. It is not always planning to the nth degree that creates the best examples of success. It can simply be an intention to do good for someone. This means using insight to know how far you intend to go. This can serve as a way for you to look into yourself and determine the parts of your 'old self' that you must let go of. It can help you gain strength for committing to a brighter future simply by envisioning it. It is almost like drawing up a plan that is not yet set in stone. It can be shaped, adapted, and reimagined because you draw upon the knowledge of your experiences. So, unify your foresight, insight, and hindsight; always learning more about yourself along the way.

My vision is to learn from my past, so that I can visualise my best self in the future.

Self-care

You have to believe in yourself when no one else does- that makes you a winner right there

Venus Williams

Notes to self:

Embrace self-love

Indulge in positive habits of mind

Uplift yourself with loving thoughts about yourself

Glorify all that you are

Discover the greatness that lies within you

Attend to your needs, wants and desires

Just do you

Nourish your soul with loving words

Treat your spirit with tenderness

Feed your body with acts of kindness

All I have to do is to be good to myself and treat myself well.

Compassion

Love and compassion are necessities, not luxuries. Without them, humanity cannot survive.

Dalai Lama

Within the fabric of my soul lies a deep quest to do good for others. I know that my inner most thoughts are considerate, loving and kind and that my smile emits such benevolence. My body language is an expression of care and compassion so that I can give of myself what others need from me to help comfort their souls. In using my voice empathetically, I provide the gateway for others to do the same. When I give my heart to those who need it most without ever expecting anything in return, I am encouraged by how much it enables them to speak love. In seeking to understand the world that others inhabit, I fully comprehend and acknowledge their struggle, loss, fear and defeat so that I may be a source of light in their lives. In speaking quietly to myself, I give the promise to care deeply about others, extending my best efforts to console their pain. When I appreciate such suffering, I understand that my greatest good must be felt from my comforting embrace. And so, I submit myself to the practice of compassion in all my relationships; spreading love wherever I may be.

I spread love for I have compassion running through my veins!

Beginning

I am starting, just where I am

Ogugua-Gee Okolo-Angus

Things to remind myself of:

- You got this
- You can
- You will
- You are able to
- You have the inner power
- You are possible
- Your adventure begins
- Your courage starts
- Your stepping out is right here
- You have the tools
- You can picture your success
- You are making a way
- You have found a way
- You are amazingly gifted- always believe it!

Go forth, you are ready to make your mark in this world!

Interpretation

You must never be fearful about what you are doing when it is right

Rosa Parks

Steps for success:

1. Interpret your surroundings consciously, using positive energy as your reality
2. Use your wisdom, recognising it as the interpretation of your experiences
3. Know that your words are powerful so recognise how they will be interpreted
4. Look through hidden occurrences and find the truth behind subtle messages
5. Beware of the conscious habits of mind so that you interpret your experiences meaningfully through powerful thoughts
6. Use repeated positive interpretations as the wisdom for understanding
7. Guide your thoughts consciously about how you view the world
8. Remember your thoughts are interpretations of the decisions you make
9. Your knowledge of self allows you to change the meaning of your experiences

Your interpretations create your reality- keep them encouraging

Self- image

You are your greatest hero

Unknown

Your special gifts and talents enable you to make a difference in other people's lives. Trust yourself to tell your heart how brilliant, awesome, and fabulous you are. Your mind matters and in feeding it with positive thoughts you continuously develop your self-image. Minding your emotional diet enables you to draw healthy conclusions about your strength. Acceptance of oneself means you can look deeply into your soul and feel contented. Understanding and accepting your greatness enlightens your heart and helps you shine like the star you were meant to be. When nurturing a positive self-image, you unconditionally give permission for others to do the same. Falling in love with who you are is the greatest fulfilment of peace. In making a commitment to see yourself positively means that you make an unconscious commitment to honour yourself even if no one else does. So, go forth and be your greatest hero! This is really where it starts. Empower your mind, body, and soul by affirming your greatness. Trust your heart with positive thoughts about yourself so that they become the fabric of your soul. Be the very best example of yourself because you are amazing! Always remember that!

Each and every day I will honour all that I am and all that I am becoming. I will build the best possible image of myself.

Diplomacy

Diplomacy is the art of letting someone else have your way

Proverb

You are the deciding instrument. You hold the position of responsibility. You set the direction. You determine the outcome. But you need people to share your vision. And so, as you develop the art of diplomacy you represent an idea that others think is theirs. You project your vision in such a way that others believe they created it. You make your mark in this world by giving the toughest messages with love! You create the climate for change without ever offending anyone. You got tact. You got style. You got presence. You delicately deal with issues head on but in your insightful way you resolve conflict. You limit your judgments always remembering the power you hold for making peace. You are insightful and this enables you to perceptively dampen all fires before they ignite. You are the peacemaker. You are the advocate for change always mediating the message so that it rests comfortably in the hearts and minds of those who need it most. You pacify the pressure because you know that it is not everything you think that you always have to say. You have discovered how to remain principled, very principled as an arbitrator for social justice and equality. You are the cause of all things good in our society.

I will always remain hopeful that we can resolve our differences by finding the middle ground. That is the strength of diplomacy.

Encouragement

I can avail myself to extraordinary things

Lupita Nyong'o

Our greatest good is the good we give to ourselves. Let our hearts be that which keeps us motivated and encouraged even in the toughest of times. Wherever we are now at this very moment let us speak to our hearts. We all know that life throws us a curve ball at times. That curve ball is deliberate. It sometimes gives us the lessons we need to hear about ourselves. Often it throws us off our intended path, if only to protect us from the damage we may do to ourselves. At other times it serves to remind us of our extraordinary strength. It serves to teach us that we should never put limitations on our capacity to be great, to live great and to do great things. The curve ball is the guiding light for reminding us that we are our own kind of amazing. It motivates us to speak positive words over ourselves and to use them in the most profound way. The praise and encouragement we give to ourselves must overwhelm our doubt, fear, or chaos. We learn that in order to give to others we must give to ourselves the encouragement to overcome challenges. For we know the power of positive thoughts that manifest in positive actions and meaningful messages about how we show up in the world.

Today, we each make our promise to develop a positive mindset that will direct our path to our achievements.

Fulfilment

Life is more meaningful when our goal is fulfilment rather than gratification

Unknown

This is what I know:

- You can find ways to ensure that your life is fulfilled, so you won't feel the need to gravitate to people who do not serve you well
- Self-fulfilment is your life work for living in peace so that you focus on your own happiness
- You are the decision maker and with that knowledge you develop the opportunities you wish to create for yourself
- There are many different roads to fulfilment and as long as yours is authentic you will never get lost
- Self-love, self-care, and self-reliance will contribute to your self-fulfilment
- You are your greatest teacher for communicating how you need to be fulfilled
- Sometimes all we need is some encouragement to decide our next steps in order to travel on the path to finding the very thing that satisfies our soul

I seek nothing other than to be fulfilled and I shall meditate in the fullness of making that happen.

Perseverance

The best way to lift one's self up is to help someone else

Booker T. Washington

Your role as a teacher is magnificent because you transform the lives of children. You do not stop; you do not give in and you do not give up. Your great work is performed with persistence, insistence, and integrity. You persevere even in the most challenging of times and stupendously provide the positive climate for learning. Your tenacious spirit is evident as you navigate your teaching through external pressures; always keeping going. The fact that you are still in the profession, makes us know of your commitment to improvement. You have never been limited by your circumstances and that makes such a difference in your classroom. You push on, you stay true to your goals, always making a total effort to do your best. Whatever you are going through takes a back seat because you are always prepared to finish what you have started. You never put limits on the work you have to do, and the results are attained because of your unwavering dedication. You find the strength within you no matter what because of your heartfelt promise to carry the burdens for the children whom you love.

You are appreciated for your perseverance in doing what really matters.

Preparedness

Fortune favours the prepared mind

Louis Pasteur

Your role as a teacher exemplifies:

- Survival strategies for coping with the continuous demands that teaching brings
- Readiness to accept challenges, seeing them as obstacles to overcome
- Combating negativity and inequality because you know how many lives would be lost
- Preparation for battle against the odds for all children in your care
- A strategic approach for handling any unexpected learning experiences
- Setting direction so that you can prepare for the future
- Strategically thinking through your plans so that they manifest into decisive actions
- Strategically planning your approach so that you prepare for all eventualities as best as you can
- Strategically influencing in your immediate environment thus providing memorable learning experiences
- Steadying your nerves when all around you are losing theirs

You are prepared, you are ready, and you take no chances.

Values

When your values are clear to you, making decisions becomes easier

Roy E. Disney

The commitment you exemplify in your teaching is one of the purest examples of the value you place for doing your life work. The behaviours you demonstrate are reflections of all that you believe in. Your personal conviction is consistent with your moral code of fairness and equity. You are honourable, trustworthy, and genuine and this transmits through your teaching. You care deeply about the difference you are making, and you are clear as to why that is necessary. You focus on never ending self-improvement to encourage the development of others. In this way, there is alignment between what you feel, say, and do. You make values-based choices that are shaped by your integrity. Your mission aligns the 'why', the 'what' and the 'how' in your daily teaching practices.

Your teaching is from the depths of your soul and it shows up so purposefully.

Vision

Whatever we believe about ourselves and our ability comes true for us

Susan L Taylor

Keep believing in your dreams and never ever give up on them. Remember the desires of your heart. Keep working on the things you believe in because your conscious thoughts will keep you going. Use your foresight for shaping what you wish for your future. Articulate your vision in ways that make sense to you. Relentlessly drive through the obstacles as you achieve much learning along the way. Trust the process that will ensure your vision is realised in the way it is intended. Even if people put limitations on your goals, believe that your imagination will carry you far. So, dare to dream because this is the reality you create for yourself.

Wherever you go, keep your vision alive in your mind!

Significance

It is what difference we have made to the lives of others that will determine the significance of the life we lead

Nelson Mandela

You know what really matters to you. The things that are important are those that you work hard for. Your actions are characterised not only because of what you do, but importantly by the difference you make. You show up in the world as a true reflection of the values you hold. You are willing to keep trying to be better so that you can do better. Your significant contribution to this world reflects the number of children you have made smile. There is never a time when you decide to quit. In your own small, yet significant way, you touch a soul and warm a heart with your steadfast love that can be depended upon. The significant part you play is making others stronger. And as such, you are the greatest manifestation of goodness and dignity.

You have created the climate for thinking great, being great and doing great!

Responsive to need

If a curriculum does not respond to a culture, then the culture won't respond to the curriculum

Leslie Hooks

As an educator who cares so deeply about the success of others:

- I am responsive to need
- I am in the fight for social change
- My moral compass is pointing in the right direction
- I am a change agent who intervenes at the point of need
- I am responsive to change
- I am encouraging culturally responsive learning
- I am responsive to all colours of the rainbow and those in between
- I am responsive in my promotion of social justice and equity
- My strategic influence is making a positive difference
- I am responsive to my students' needs and do all that I can from my heart

I accept my power and the responsibility that comes with reconstructing and building a meaningful curriculum.

Entitlement

Where there is inequality, I promise you I will change the narrative

Ogugua-Gee Okolo-Angus

A reminder:

Dear children of my heart, you came into this world and watched the adults make decisions for the life you would become. You had no control but to accept the circumstances you were born into. Today I learnt that for some of you these situations are less than ideal. It broke my heart to learn of your suffering. My teaching will make a difference so that you recognise the gifts you were born with. The lessons I create and deliver will enable you to truly understand your greatness. The daily messages I give to you will reinforce the commitment I have made for ensuring your success. You are deserving of so much and I know the role I must play in shaping what you can and will become. I recognise the importance of my role and I will not let you down. You are deserving of a life fulfilled and my influence will ensure you experience the life you need, want and desire.

By planning, reviewing, adapting, and modifying the lessons I will teach, I ensure that children receive the most appropriate learning experience they are entitled to.

Being Assertive

If you don't like something change it. If you can't change it, change your attitude

Maya Angelou

Conscious Conversations:

I must have courage to ask for what I want. In making my requests I only intend to experience things that serve me well. My ultimate feeling of freedom rests within me. It is my responsibility for ensuring that nothing interrupts the positive energy that flows within me. I am clear about what I want for myself and I intend to pursue it; always being mindful about how I make others feel. This is supporting me to recognise my potential for speaking up for myself. I will continue to illuminate myself by raising my words and not my voice. This is giving me the courage to be a true reflection of my inner being. It is now possible to say no to things I do not feel is good for my soul without feeling guilty. This is making me much more open to express how I feel. I am fine to make difficult choices because I am courageous. I am learning the art of asserting myself positively, so it is clear who I am and the person I am becoming.

This is the permission I am giving myself and I am sticking with it!

Commitment

Changing the narrative in our education system is a relentless commitment worth undertaking

Ogugua-Gee Okolo-Angus

Teacher Voices:

- Commitment to progress
- Commitment to change for the better
- Commitment to making a difference
- Commitment to success for children
- Commitment to focusing on the good I can do
- Commitment to focusing on the barriers I will break
- Commitment to hard work
- Commitment to selfless work
- Commitment to improving lives
- Commitment to transformation where it is most needed

I encourage a shared commitment to education reform as a deliberate act that will make a difference.

Courage

Courage may be the most important of all virtues, because without it one cannot practice any other virtue with consistency

Maya Angelou

If all things around you seem to diminish the work you are trying to do, have courage to stand tall, stand firm and assert your truth. Know that in times of resistance, you must be honest with yourself, believing that what you are seeking to put right is worth pursuing. As you hold the future of children and young people in your hands, commit to courage. In your moment of truth, summon the courage to go against the grain even where there is challenge. It might make you feel uncomfortable at first, but in doing so will make you will feel proud in using your fighting spirit, so that your voice can be heard and the children and young people in your care benefit greatly.

It is with conviction and determination that I will stand firm in what I believe in, knowing that I am a vital element of children and young people's success.

Choices

Choices are the hinges of destiny

Edwin Markham

We make choices when entering the teaching profession. We decide how to design our classrooms, creating a purposeful atmosphere within the learning space. We plan how to deliver our curriculum; we choose how to inject energy and passion. It seems obvious therefore that when we realise that children and young people need our teachings, we choose to be a force for good. We take decisions for making our teaching the best it can be. We know that the conscious choices we make will enable us to deliver the education in a way that matters most to children and young people we serve.

Today, is a day in which I will recognise the conscious choices I can make so that children and young people in my care can thrive everyday they enter my classroom.

Kindness

Your gift of kindness is free

Solomon Obiajulu Okolo

Has there ever been a time when you decided to give some of your time to support someone who needed help? What did that feel like? Did you make them see the best in themselves? Did you make them feel encouraged? As a wise man once said, kindness that comes from your heart, that expects nothing in return is everlasting and often life changing for those who receive it. Kindness without expectation can be recognised as a selfless caring act that radiates compassion. When we acknowledge how important it is to children who have no one to love them, we better understand its purpose in our work as educators. The measure of our kindness affirms our values and our moral code.

Today I remember that kindness is one of my gifts that I happily give without expectation for anything to be returned.

Integrity

Work must be inspired by the right ideals, and education must not simply teach work, but life based on those ideals

W.E.B Du Bois

There is nothing more honourable, exacting, and necessary than integrity. And in its highest form it ensures the right things are done in the right way at the right time even when no one is looking. As the teacher who will forever leave an imprint in the souls of children' hearts just know that you are the deciding instruments of their future. That is why your actions and thoughts must be based upon your values of honesty and integrity. And as you step out into the classroom with the children you care so deeply about your soul must consciously have its own set of rules that favours social justice, equity and fairness despite what is going on in the world. This is to ensure that every fibre of your being treats all children and young people with the same highest regard despite any circumstances they were born into.

Today I choose to honour all children and young people that I serve as I ensure that they are all provided with the same equality of opportunity regardless of circumstance.

Patience

Patience is the calm acceptance that things can happen in a different order than the one you have in mind

Anon

You have a plan. You work hard to develop a lesson that is stimulating, engaging and meaningful. From where you are positioned the teaching of this lesson should go according to what was intended. But what if it does not? What then? What now? How might you respond. Patience is an important pause in the process of teaching. For it will allow you to quash your frustrations and by its virtue plant the seeds of tolerance and understanding. And in this way, it will support the way you will observe your thoughts so that you may reorder your actions. Patience will be your powerful companion to peace you will feel when you realign your plans. In its most elegant form, patience you feel will be the wisdom you will exemplify; demonstrating that in life, plans sometimes unfold in their own way at their own time.

On this day, I will take some time to be still. I will commit to nullifying any frustrations I might feel for exercising patience.

Love

The only way to do great work is to love what you do

Steve Jobs

Love the skin you are in! That is an essential ingredient in your life work. Seek to find that inner love that shines its light on peace, harmony, and tranquillity. Let your love be the light in this world that creates your expression of hope. Let the significant portion of your day, week and year that is taken up by your work be filled with love. Let love reign in your life and in its purest form restore and heal any broken system. And as matters of the heart, let love awaken your soul and deepen your unshakeable belief that the only way to do your great work is to love what you do.

For me to love my work, I must first love myself. For me to do great work, so too must I be great. My greatness comes from loving all that I am and all that I am becoming.

Conscious Commitments

Commitment

Our conscious acts are needed for a desired experience

Ogugua-Gee

Commit to the actions you will take for getting to know and appreciate your inner self. Commit to finding solutions to challenges that are burdensome. Commit to transforming your role as an educator, just because you can. Commit your heart to supporting the development of children and young people in the most productive way possible. Commit to motivating yourself, even in the hardest of times. Commit to the promises you made for the good of all children. Commit with purpose. Commit with love. Commit with care. Consciously commit to doing the right thing in the right way at the right time. Commit with all that you know and with all that you have.

I commit my power behind my declaration for creating an experience that is good for myself and others.

Self-Worth

There are no pre-requisites for worthiness

Brene Brown

Do you really know the strength of your inner power? Always believe that you are that special type of greatness. Make self-honouring choices as your gateway to fulfilment. Be your own kind of beautiful and own all aspects of your life and the decisions you take. Be good to yourself and this will be reflected onto others. For every situation, reclaim your worthiness if you feel it slipping away. That is your right. Stand in the skin you are in and compare yourself to the reflection in the mirror and accept that you were born worthy. When you give yourself permission to live in that way, you will never have to convince others of your worthiness for it lives within you and permeates in all that you do.

I am my greatest hero. No one but me can destroy my feeling of self-worth. I am the deciding instrument for positively shaping all things in my life.

Acceptance

Self-acceptance our pathway to peace

Ogugua-Gee Okolo-Angus

You are the best example of yourself. In this very moment accept all that you are and all that you emit into the world. For it is with this acceptance of self that you can hold up the mirror and truly identify your greatness. Knowing that you were destined to make a positive difference to the children and young people whose lives you touch each day, provides the best reason for accepting just how intelligent, knowledgeable, and smart you are. Your role as a teacher defines this in so many ways. You not only impart knowledge through your teaching, but you also transform lives by forever leaving your mark in the world and importantly in the hearts and minds of those who trust you most. Accept that your path was directed in such a way for making a difference because you carry the responsibility of holding children's lives in your hands.

I accept myself for all that I am and all that I am becoming. I understand that my self-reflection supports my personal and professional progress so that I can be my best and do my best.

Triumph

I learned that courage was not the absence of fear but triumph over it

Nelson Mandela

Note to self:

1. I am a champion of all things equitable and fair
2. My triumph comes because I am relentlessly focused
3. My experiences have taught me that endurance creates success
4. I am courageous and that gives me strength
5. My difficulties have helped me to bounce back, and shine through
6. My bravery has meant that I have conquered my battles
7. I realise that my positive mindset has kept me going
8. My accomplishments are the chances I took
9. The fear I had no longer exists
10. My can-do approach has brought light to darkness

When I try and try and try and try, I eventually triumph!

Social justice is the Change Agent

Never stop wanting to build a better world

Mary McLeod Bethune

We must continue to fight with all our might because truth is all we have. We must accept the words of Dr Martin King and acknowledge that "injustice anywhere is a threat to justice everywhere". Until such time we cannot rest because those who are underprivileged need our voices and actions to represent them purposefully. Where we witness gross inequality, we must call it out for what it is. Our greatest trigger for doing our work as change agents is because other people matter. We cannot afford to feel the depths of despair for our work is far too important. When we care deeply, we continue to give much of ourselves and that will surely make a difference. We are restless and seek to witness positive change where it is needed. We commit ourselves because we are filled with a sense of responsibility for others.

I carry the burdens of the voiceless so that they may be listened to, valued, and heard!

Change Agent Impact

You were made for impact

Ogugua-Gee Okolo-Angus

I create all opportunities for doing a great job

I am excellent

I have an abundance of talents

Greatness surrounds me

I am recognised for the positive contributions I make

I accept myself and all that I do

I am the deciding instrument for change

My power is evident, and I use it responsively

Every part of me is positive

I radiate courage and optimism

I am making a long-lasting positive contribution in this world.

Purposeful Life

The purpose of life is to live it, to taste experience to the utmost

Eleanor Roosevelt

My life is fulfilled and that makes me happy with all that I experience. I believe in greatness and this propels me to do good for others. My life has meaning, and I am glad to be alive. There is passion and purpose in my life that ignites all possibilities. I am recognising my gifts of greatness and how to use them to shape the world. Optimism stays with me no matter the challenges I may face. I take my responsibilities seriously, recognising the power I hold. I am blessed with gifts and talents that I am happy to share with the world. I add meaning to my life when I reach out and touch a life. I set my intentions clearly and work towards achieving my goals. I am on a mission and have no time to be idle. I am living beyond my current experiences and using them as stepping-stones to success. My purposeful life is doing good where it matters most.

Today, I recognise the impact I am making and the sense of purpose it adds to my existence.

Accountable

A man who stands for nothing will fall for everything

Malcolm X

Teacher voices:

- I am accountable for the planning I decide upon for each lesson I teach
- I am accountable for the classroom climate I create
- I am accountable for the resources I use to stimulate children's minds
- I am accountable for my style of questioning I use to encourage and uplift
- I am responsible for the way I deliver my lessons to include all children equally
- I am responsible for understanding children's needs, wants and desires
- I am accountable for finding solutions to support children on their journey
- I am responsible for motivating children to be the best they can be
- I am responsible for creating a culture of integrity and openness
- I am accountable for taking decisive actions to remove all forms of injustice

I hold myself accountable for doing good in the world.

Conscious Commitment

Visibility

... and that visibility which makes us most vulnerable is that which is also the source of our greatest strength

Audre Lorde

Notes to self:

I must:

Never underestimate the power of my visibility

Continue to emit my personal power

Be my true authentic self

Show up in the world positively

Make waves so people know I am here

Be courageous so others know what I stand for

Make my truth visible

Encourage self-assertiveness

Trust my instincts and make my voice heard

I promise to keep my light glowing but never to dim the light in others.

Thinking Smart

Make more moves and less announcements

Twenty20

How many of us are often screaming inside whilst appearing calm on the outside? How many of us dim our light so others can shine? Do we give to others all of ourselves to the point of exhaustion? How many times have we celebrated the achievements of others; barely acknowledging our own? When did we last give ourselves a break from the perpetual work we do? When will we decide to think smart, be smart and work smart?

Can we agree that before we can work smart, we must think smart? Can we recognise that before we can diminish the strain we place upon our shoulders, that we must devise a smart plan? Can we acknowledge the fact that we before we can lessen the constant flow of work, we have to set our intentions rightly?

To work smart, be smart and act smart we must think smart!

Preparation

The future belongs to those who prepare for it today

Malcolm X

You use your gift of greatness to prepare the path so that your students can experience all things positive. Your teaching is instrumental in shaping hearts and minds so that your children are taught how to think. You create the future because you know how to engage them so purposefully. The decisions you make in your teaching provides the platform for students to determine what they are capable of achieving. You never stop even when you are tired because you recognise your work is never done. You are the best example of a positive self-image and you exemplify this in your classroom. The steps you make for ensuring success often takes you out of your comfort zone but that never deters you. You do not expect anything to manifest, you prepare for it; never taking anything for granted. And in each step, you celebrate your children's successes- every milestone that prepares the ground for their lives to be well lived.

You are great in all dimensions as you purposefully plan for children to achieve.

Mind- Matters

Those who mind don't matter and those that matter don't mind

Dr Seuss

This is what I have come to learn:

- The power of your mind can transform all things into possibility
- Your mind is the mental matter that will forever determine your pathway
- You have the power to change all of your thoughts for the better
- It begins with your thought and extends to your actions- so make them worthwhile
- As you get wiser you realise what matters to your mind
- A healthy mindset is the fuel you need to feed your body
- Vibrations of your mind connect to the vibrations of your heart- keep them positive
- Your attitude reflects the matters of your mind
- Your disposition reflects the matters of your mind
- You have to be kind to your mind

What you dwell on today will manifest into existence- I am keeping it positive!

Hard Work

Everything you have done and been through is important

Iyanla Vanzant

Your hard work, dedication and commitment has not gone unnoticed. You always make time in your day to support those who still need your help. You never stop and this is because you commit to your cause. You always achieve what you work for because you think big. You feel a sense of achievement because amazing things are happening in the children whom you serve so well. You never stop even when you are tired. You know nothing comes easy but that does not deter you. You do your job well always making sure it matters. You are being rewarded for all of the efforts you make. Your willingness to work hard is a driving force that gets you results. You recognise opportunity in hard work. You know the benefits of hard work because you are at it all the time. And even when you feel that you cannot go on, you realise the demonstrable difference you are making.

I pledge to continue my hard work for creating success for others.

All is well

Everything is working out for my highest good

Louise Hay

Today I affirm to myself:

- I attract all that is positive
- Out of every situation, I find peace
- My mind is clear
- I am no longer struggling with things I cannot manage
- My heart is full
- I dwell on all things great
- I am strong enough to deal with challenges
- Everything is turning out great
- My life is full of joy
- I am surrounded by all things wonderful

All is well in my heart, body, and soul.

Inspiration

The road to success is always under construction

Steve Harvey

This is what I realise:

- I am all things great if only I allow myself to think that way
- No-one can dim my light or steal my thunder unless I give them permission
- I am the best contributor to my peaceful state of mind
- I know that I must trust my inner self and trust my heart and soul for it knows best
- Today is another opportunity for me to be the best example of myself
- Gratitude is an act I must practice daily
- I am my greatest hero
- I have no regrets only learning experiences
- I can re-write any chapter of my life so that it is filled with goodness
- I can be strong even in the face of pain and adversity

Today I am making clear and conscious choices to be an inspiration to those around me and to myself.

Support

I want you to know that someone out there cares

Unknown

You don't have to say

- We hear you

You don't have to act

- We see you

You don't have to worry

- We feel you

You need not despair

- We got you

You do not have to ask

- We answered you

You do not have to be alone

- We stand with you

You do not have to be silenced

- We champion all that you are and the good that you are doing in this world

We surround you with love and encouragement.

Excellence

We need to internalise this idea of excellence

Barack Obama

In the pursuit of excellence, we must keep trying things to see if they work. We have to do all we can to make sure our children do all they can. It is not by accident that we have to make a sincere effort to skilfully create opportunities for others. We visualise obstacles as the opportunities we need to keep us moving. We have to be prepared to build excellence in our lives. We have to do this by developing positive daily habits that improve our efforts to do good. By doing what we do repeatedly we must continue our sincere efforts to shine the light for others. Our commitment to building hope is rooted in our determination to do the best we can.

We are pursuing excellence with all our passion and it sure is worth it!

Empathy

I see you; I hear you; I got you

Ogugua-Gee Okolo-Angus

Teachers Thoughts:

I know your troubles- **I am here for you**

I understand what you are going through- **I will help you**

I realise how much you are doing- **I understand your intentions**

You need my strength- **I will not let you fall**

As you go through your challenges-**I will hold your hand**

I hold compassion for you in my heart-**I will never let you suffer**

I am getting to understand your situation -**So that I can capture your pain**

I feel your pain in my soul-**I got you**

I am respectful of your struggles- **I make no judgements**

I want to continue to connect with you- **I commit to you wholeheartedly**

I am aware- I hear you, I see you, I got you!

Co-operation

Progress is the attraction that moves humanity

Marcus Garvey

Our combined efforts will do good for others who so desperately need us. Intentional actions will ensure we keep going even through the difficulties. In understanding how we each work together; we can serve others better. We realise that there must be things we must be willing to sacrifice so that we can accomplish all that we set out to do. Our belief is that we all get there when everyone gets there, and we must create the climate for this to happen. In this way we help to develop creative talents that may otherwise go unnoticed. Together we are powerful, and it is in our cooperation that our collective constructive efforts become a force for good.

Our greatest cooperative efforts are for the greater good of humanity!

Adaptability

We cannot direct the wind, but we can adjust the sails

Dolly Parton

- I can adjust to any situation because I manage change well
- I have developed a flexible mindset so that I remain open to new experiences
- I am willing to change where necessary because I remain curious
- I can adapt to situations because I have developed wisdom to see things differently
- I readily make changes in my life which creates memorable learning opportunities
- I am happy to move on because I have the capacity to do so
- I can modify my approach even where there is uncertainty
- I am capable of unfixing my set patterns because I can look outside of my immediate situation
- I am fine to let go of certainty so that I can embrace new possibilities
- My risk-taking approach to learning is creating more opportunities for me

I have learnt the key to change is to be willing!

Change Agents make positive contributions

Nothing changes if nothing changes

Unknown

Your contribution as a change agent means that you:

- Are fearless
- Take your responsibility seriously
- Accomplish all that you set out to do
- Believe you can
- Surrender what is no longer important or necessary
- Lead from the front, lead from the back, lead anywhere necessary
- Always show up
- Understand your service role
- Are flexible but firm because of your beliefs
- Know that it is worth it

I am always reminded that it is never too late to be a change agent!

Knowledge

Teaching is more than imparting knowledge; it is inspiring change. Learning is more than absorbing facts; it is acquiring understanding.

William Arthur Ward

Imparting knowledge is the basic action that seeks to advance children and young people. In its most liberating form, this process has no end. It furnishes the minds of young and old, creating the climate for progress. When we build genuine learning opportunities, we help to inspire change by creating possibilities. We must however understand that we require the methods, tools, and dispositions to do it just right. Imparting knowledge must be purposefully planned with precision. When we look deep within ourselves, we can organise our thoughts and behaviours once we accept our duty as role models. In this way, as teachers we have a profound positive impact in the world in which we instil the love of learning in the hearts and minds of children we care so deeply about.

On this day, I pledge to focus on the job of inspiring young minds so that they can love learning and create their own pathways to success.

Conscious Commitment

Change Agents take Conscious Actions

Consciousness is an attitude of the mind

Steve Biko

As a Change Agent I take clear and conscious actions to:

Speak my mind and speak the truth

Walk positively with purpose

Stay focused

Keep standing

Keep pushing on

Solve problems

Commit to change

Challenge the stereotypes

Learn lessons and move forwards

Consciously condition my mind to do great work

I strategically manage my mind so that good thoughts always flow from it!

Loyalty

Loyalty is a decision, a resolution of the soul

Pascal Mercier

Thank you for the:

- Strong support you give
- Honesty you live by
- Trust you engender
- Patience you demonstrate
- Truth you project
- Faith you live by
- Hope you hold onto
- Courage you show
- Morals you live by
- Dignity you create
- Love and light, you bring into other people's lives

Thank you for pledging your truth and sticking by it!

Equity is in a Change Agent

If you have only one smile in you, give it to the people you love

Maya Angelou

As a Change Agent I always:

- Show respect
- Give respect
- Treat everyone fairly
- Accept everyone for who they are
- Uplift and empower
- Uncomplicate equality
- Recognise greatness
- Liberate
- Stand up for justice
- Lead where it matters

I am not afraid of my role as a change agent because it is way too important!

First Steps

You do not have to see the whole staircase just to take the first step

Dr Martin Luther King

- Student: Miss, I just cannot do this
- Teacher: Do not be troubled for I am here to support you
- Student: But I still cannot see a way through
- Teacher: Start small, start where you are, but just start, I got you
- Student: I am trying now but it doesn't seem as if I am getting there
- Teacher: It is all part of your learning so feel your fear, recognise, and acknowledge it
- Student: Ok, I am afraid to take this massive leap into the unknown
- Teacher: I got you, I am walking with you
- Student: I feel your strength, thank you
- Teacher: That's your inner strength, your voice telling you that you can
- Student: I am holding onto my faith that I will make it
- Teacher: That's because you recognise the problem and are finding the solution
- Student: I realise that in order to do this I have to prepare my mind
- Teacher: You cannot see what is around the corner but now you have reimagined possibilities
- Student: I have, I have! I now know that to get to the things I want, I have to decide how I go about it.

Teacher: I recognise that your first step will be the hardest, but your journey to fulfilment will be possible when you close the door on past negative thoughts and step into a new beginning.

Conscious Commitment

Education

Education is the most powerful weapon which you can use to change the world

Nelson Mandela

When Malcolm X said that ''education is the passport to the future'', he wisely reminded us of how it will direct our lives and determine our opportunities. If Dr Martin Luther King could be heard today, we would accept his words in which ''intelligence plus character is the goal of true education''. If we recognise the power in Oprah Winfrey's voice, we will accept it when she says for ''every one of us that succeeds, it's because there's somebody out there to show you the way out''. If we remember that inequalities still exist, we will endorse the feelings of Shirley Chisholm who was only too ''aware that tremendous amounts of talent are being lost to our society just because the talent wears a skirt''. In advocating for an education system that is fair and just we value the words of Dr Martin Luther King who purports that ''our lives begin to end the day we become silent about things that matter''. And when we want to comfort our hearts, we hold on the words of B.B. King and acknowledge ''the beautiful thing about learning is nobody can take it away from you''. When we know who we are and recognise our power we can support James Baldwins notion that ''not everything that is faced can be changed but nothing can be changed until it is faced''. When we know who we are and believe it we can accept James Baldwin's belief that ''the purpose of education is to create in a person the ability to look at the world for himself [herself] to make his [her] own decisions. And as Barack Obama so aptly suggested ''change will not come if we wait for some other person or some other time. We are the ones we've been waiting for. We are the change we seek''. And that is simply how it is.

I shall continue to use my voice, my platform, my presence to be the force for change so that no child will ever be disadvantaged because of the education they receive.

Decisions

Always make decisions that prioritise your inner peace

Izey Victoria Odiase

Note to self:

Make life changing decisions that ensure your peace

Commit your decisions to the desires of your heart

Do the right thing at the right time in the right way because you know it must be done

Make clear and conscious choices to do good for yourself and others

Make firm choices that lead you to stay true to your values

Make a conscious decision to stay focused on our goals recognising the importance of this

Make decisions by listening to your heart

Make decisions by listening to your soul

Make choices for letting love in

Make a commitment, then follow it up and follow it through

Make it! Do it! Be it! See it! Feel it!

Collaboration

I need to you, you need me, together we can live in harmony

Ogugua-Gee Okolo-Angus

I need you. You need me. We need each other. Let's make our collaboration a priority. Let's build it upon love, care, and compassion. Together we can do so much. Together we can be so much. I commit to you. You commit to me. We commit to each other. We recognise the strength of our union and find ways to make it work. We tune into the silent processes that bind our hearts together. We share the same stage. We stand on the same platform, equally, appreciating the power of our purpose together. We capture each other's gifts and use them collectively for the greater good. We are a source of inspiration that enables our hearts to connect. We are the dream team that recognises the beauty of our association. We have trust, love, understanding and faith that our union will stand the test of time. We learn from each other because we give our equal share to our collaboration. We swear allegiance in that our partnership goals are those that endorse convergence in a world where competition predominates. When we take this stance, we commit our hearts and minds into a deep sense of consciousness that gives true meaning to cooperation and communication.

Let us be the powerful force we have always been destined to be. Let us celebrate the goodness of our union.

Self-Reliance

I don't have any limitations on what I think I could do or be

Oprah Winfrey

The Self-Reliance plan:

I. Trust the instinctive nature of your soul
II. Decide what you intend to do or to be
III. Insist on your uniqueness
IV. Do what is worthy for your soul
V. Lead with conviction, courage, and confidence
VI. Protect the sacred integrity of your heart
VII. Take on the responsibility for directing your own path
VIII. Affirm your greatness then prove it
IX. Be a demonstration of your heart's desires
X. Start where you are and do all that you can

My goal is to remind myself that I am my greatest asset.

Optimism

A good teacher can inspire hope, ignite the imagination, and instil a love of learning

Brad Henry

Always remain optimistic for it is the faith that holds you tightly when the world is caving in. Believing you are about to experience something wonderful will make you feel better in the end. Finding ways to explore solutions is the key for never giving up. Keeping focused on your goals and objectives is a great way for seeing opportunity in every difficulty. For whatever is meant for us will never pass us by. As educators we must inject optimism into our hearts, thus choosing to see beyond our circumstances.

Dream your wildest dreams but make a realistic assessment of where you are in your life. This will support you in your quest for keeping positive. We become the definition of how we handle struggles and what we decide to hold onto. When we confidently believe we have the power to change the world, we give ourselves the possibility of seeing it manifest. We recognise this courage as progress, and it supports our relentless drive to make a long-lasting difference to the children in our care.

My thoughts are simple: keep positive, be positive, do positive and we shall achieve our greatest glory.

Conscious Commitment

Fresh Start

A bird sitting in a tree is never afraid of branch breaking, because it's trust is not in the branch, it is in its wings

Unknown

This is what I have learnt:

- Sometimes it is essential to let go
- Pain is not perpetual and does not last forever
- It is a new day to commit to growing from painful experiences
- Life is full of possibilities
- Every day is a new beginning
- It is never too late
- You can re-create your situation into the best you need it to be
- Starting again is a process
- Your journey to happiness requires a purposeful plan
- There are no rules as to how to make yourself happy and at peace

Today I commit to my fresh start and the opportunities it will bring.

Motivation

Get up, stand up, stand up for your rights

Bob Marley

What I have come to believe in is:

My power

My greatness

My gifts

My strength

My self-knowledge

My imagination

My talents

My blessings

My successes

My sparkle

Note to self: how my greatness is perceived by others is none of my business for I am just doing me!

Assertiveness

Assertiveness is not what you do, it's who you are!

Shakti Gawain

Today I choose to develop the right mental attitude so that my measure of self-control and assertiveness is in balance. Today I give myself permission to go forth and seek justice. I recognise that I may be pushed back or silenced but I am choosing to relax into the idea that my voice must be heard. And in valuing myself, I am choosing to assert my hearts desires so that I may know peace. I am choosing to acknowledge and accept the challenges that stand in my way. For it is now that I recognise them as simply obstacles to overcome. I am proclaiming positive words and actions in a way that asserts all that I stand for and all that I am. I am certainly strong, bold, and courageous yet caring and considerate. I am choosing to present myself to the world as a formidable human being that advocates for social justice. I am training my mind to overcome fear so that I may project my self-assertive character into the world. I am choosing to stand in a space that radiates conscious, wise, and thoughtful decisions that help others become the very best example of themselves. Eloquently and courageously, I am taking a stand for doing good for myself and others.

I recognise the power and purpose of being assertive and I know how to do this positively.

Inner Peace

Do not let the behaviour of others destroy your inner peace

Dalai Lama

This is what I believe:

That my inner peace is my absolute priority

Somewhere deep within me is the golden silence that comforts my heart

My private life is my peaceful life

Being still, really still and listening to my breath brings peace to my body

Inner peace is the greatest reward I can give to myself

It is I who must cultivate a positive mindset to experience harmony

It is I who must prioritise the things that elevate my happiness

It is I who must embrace all things tranquil into my life

It is I who must remind myself daily of my gifts and talents

It is I who must remember that I am priceless and precious

Today I commit to a life filled with inner peace so that I remove negativity out of my existence.

Abundance

Doing what you love is the cornerstone for having abundance in your life

Wayne Dyer

What is the secret to living an abundant life full of joy? How might I go about my daily duties creating peace within in my soul? How can I diminish the limitations put upon me through limitless thoughts that help me fly? Why must I continue to be grateful so as to attract positive things into my life? How can I continue to focus on the successes in my life? What are the ways for learning about the virtues of abundance so that I may be inspired to open the door into endless possibilities? How can I ensure I remain open to receive all opportunities that have been afforded to me? How can I live fully, being present in the richness of all things I experience? How can I make sure that I am always of benefit to others? What can I do to continue to live my life in abundance because I am open and ready to receive it in my life?

I choose to give to others unconditionally hoping that they will experience good things in abundance.

Possibility

Ask for what you want and be prepared to get it

Maya Angelou

Into my heart I commit all things so that I may see things as they really are. Into my life I commit to actions in that I may focus on endless possibilities that await me. Into my thoughts I commit to the belief that I am powerful beyond measure. Into my soul I search for the infinite possibilities that surround me. Into my dreams I submit to the greatness that comes from believing I will do good for others. Into my mind I dwell in perpetual possibility. I no longer compare myself to others. I keep believing that being fully present to my thoughts will magnify and help me reach my goals. I take nothing for granted and know that patience will bring to me all that I am deserving of. The powerful position I find myself in creates opportunities for me to do good for others. As an educator I must never doubt how far I can go so that I may open the world to the children I serve. I make space in my life so that various options can unfold. I do all that I can so that the realms of possibility follow me everywhere.

Everyday gives me an opportunity to make a difference in someone's life. With so many possibilities, I choose to be instrumental in finding a way to touch a heart.

Interaction

Every other leadership decision that must be made is seen through the lens of the impact on pupil/student learning

Reeves

We are at times shaped by the people who come into our lives. We take from our interactions all that serves us well. We know that we must make every effort to let people get close to us but managing how we do this. Human interaction must give us space to be ourselves. This helps us to become more involved and therefore contribute wherever we are more meaningfully. We must always be mindful of how we interact so that we never diminish the people around us. Connecting with others gives us the answers that may not always have been obvious. When we interact meaningfully it lets people know that we have seen them. This helps us touch a life and makes our communication stronger. In that way we make positive meaning from our interactions.

My interactions with others will be meaningful and memorable. I will continually seek to make a difference in their lives.

Change Agents

Change does not have to be hard

Iyanla Vanzant

Change Agents:

- Make clear and conscious decisions
- Are not afraid
- Have courage in the pursuit of excellence
- Are guided by their moral compass
- Knock down barriers
- Look deep within to find courage
- Advocate for reform where it is necessary
- Take decisions for the greater good
- Stand and make a demonstrable difference
- Are agents of change
- Act as catalysts in the improvement process

I am a change agent always responsive to need in our unequal society.

Gracious

Gracious words revive our spirit and restore our soul

Lailah Gifty Akita

Thank you for your:

Blessings that you pour into people's lives

Words of encouragement that you speak into the lives of children

Dreams so that you never stop trying to do good

Greatness that you radiate into the lives of others

Human acts of kindness which you demonstrate with such humility

Graciousness as you give to others unconditionally

Meaningful memories that you create in the lives of others

Confidence you exude into the world

You enrich the lives of others by the gracious gifts you bring!

Responsive

As change Agents we must always be responsive to need

Ogugua-Gee Okolo-Angus

Responsive teaching is often the weight of responsibility. It is in fact a direct call for action in which to activate our civic duties and create structures, systems and processes that are colour blind and fair. This is because we recognise the inequalities that are experienced by our children who enter our learning spaces. And so, with every decision we take, we convey our understanding of children born into circumstances far beyond their control. We hold onto this for we know the importance of our words, actions, and behaviours for making a difference. We make appropriate changes to our planning, teaching, and delivery to accommodate the differences our children project. We ensure that our learning environments are inviting and engaging so that it reinforces the holistic development of our children. When we are responsive to need, we work towards social change. When we are responsive, we find ourselves developing our teaching practice to meet the needs, wants and desires of the children whom we serve. Our stories are not always trumpet blowing instances or fist-bumping moments to celebrate. More often than not, they are quiet reflections of the significant difference we have made in our children's life simply because we are always responsive to need!

We understand the importance of our roles in doing what really matters...with purpose!

Challenge

We should always challenge was it not right... with love!

Ogugua-Gee Okolo-Angus

Stereotypes are those that often define people by the labels they have been given or stories they have been told. By challenging such things, we not only seek to change the narrative, but we defy limitations. The inequalities that exist throughout the world and also in our education system are often debilitating mechanisms of control. They can take many forms and present themselves in many ways. They may show up consciously or subconsciously but in either form they are often soul destroying. So, if you see it, hear it, feel it, or sense it, challenge it! If you know that in your role as a teacher, you affect eternity then you will equally be aware that your influence never stops. So be the change that we need to see in this uneven and unjust world. Make a difference to the children and young people who have been judged and labelled because of the circumstances they were born into. Recognise your impact in this world and dampen the fires of repression, social inequality, and ignorance. So that by your challenge, you are helping to shape a more respectful society that is more honouring and accepting of differences across the globe.

This is the day in which I commit my life work to challenging any form of prejudice. I shall do this with love in my heart and peace within my consciousness.

Persistence

Push past struggle, push past pain, push past strife no matter the strain

Ogugua-Gee Okolo-Angus

Persistence is the friendly alliance to passion and purpose. It provides the continuing course of action that keeps things moving. As long as it is purposeful, it surely will make a difference. To persist through challenges is to believe that your life work as an educator is so vitally important. Even when there are constraints, you can seek another way to conquer all things. Determining the steps, you will take to make a difference in this world can often be shaped by your relentlessness focus. So, continue to show up and make your mark. Be the enemy of resistance that holds you back from fulfilling your life work. Persevere, press on, and continue with your divine mental strength that will forever keep you encouraged.

As hard as it may be, as difficult as it may seem, I will push on and conquer for I know my life work is far too important to give in to resistance.

Responsibility

What do we live for if not to make life less difficult for others?

George Elliott

A selfless act in its simplest form is a duty that teachers uphold when entering the profession. Conscious thoughts, decisions and actions are a meaningful way for reaching out to children and young people and letting them know 'you got them'. Lovingly, this self-sacrifice is the conscious commitment you make to do good for others as you would do for yourself. This is because teachers take responsibility and live for the difference they make in other people's lives.

I accept all of the responsibility with open arms for I know the tangible difference I can make in other people's lives.

Well-Being

The greatest wealth is well-being

Lailah Gifty Akita

For a positive healthy sense of worth I choose to remember that:

- I am not in competition with anyone
- My life is good
- I have all that I need at this very moment
- Great things are manifesting in my life
- I am focused and can see my way through any difficulty
- I nurture my mind daily with positive thoughts
- I hold onto my passion, purpose and power
- I am happy, content and at peace
- I talk prosperity all of the time
- Nothing can disrupt my peace of mind
- I have no time to criticise myself

I know that my mental health is my greatest wealth.

Expectations

Other people may not have had high expectations of me....but I had high expectations of myself

Shannon Miller

In difficult times that we are living in right now, how can I keep high expectations of myself? Where there is so much negativity how must I stop blaming myself for all that bears a challenge? Why is it important to stop waiting for things if I really do not have the inner belief they will happen? What must I do to remember that being happy means having no expectations of others? How can I see that my greatness lies within me and always will? When will I stop blaming others for expecting more than I want for myself? How can I stop waiting for others to shine the light on my greatness? What must I do to ensure I live a life with no judgement or expectation? How do I set realistic expectations for myself and of myself so that it will bring me joy and comfort in challenging times? How can I remember to believe that I can, that I am able, that I have what it takes for receiving all that I desire for myself?

Today, like all days, I only have high expectations of myself.

Honesty

When you are completely honest about yourself, there is very little people can say about you that's going to have a negative impact

Charlagmane

Be still and make the effort to be honest. Work on yourself by staying true to yourself. Keep a focus on the messages you hear when you shut out the noise and there is only you standing within yourself and by yourself. Speak true of yourself even if it is uncomfortable listening. Trust your inner most voice that tells you who you are and how you are showing up in the world. Dare yourself to be the expression of your spirit because all truths are simply honest reflections of all that you are. In this way, it will never be an unpleasant listening experience because such honesty will inspire you to do better, to be better for all the children in your care. Honesty is a precious gift that we can use to make a significant contribution for a world filled with equality, peace, and love.

My honesty is my integrity, and I shall never let that diminish no matter what comes my way.

Faith

Faith is taking the first step

Martin Luther King

In times of doubt, let your heart not be troubled. Simply develop a daily mantra that motivates and encourages you to see light through darkness. Give yourself reasons to keep your faith over fear. Triumph requires you to find the belief and put your trust in something higher than yourself. To overcome any hurdles, keep your faith. Believe there are greater things to come to enable you to be of service, even when the how is unclear. Trust in all things and use your inner strength for understanding that your journey may not be easy, but it is possible. Know that there nothing in this world to prevent you from shining your light. As you make a difference to the world, worry less, and trust yourself with humble confidence. As you continue to surround your life with the grace of faith, keep believing that everything in your life becomes possible.

I look towards my faith in all things knowing I can make it through the hardest of times.

Self- Determination

One thing I have come to learn is that there is always always a way

Ogugua-Gee Okolo-Angus

Best examples to determine your positive pathway in life:

- Have an honest conversation with your heart and mind
- Know your strengths and use them as your driver
- Set clear intentions for success
- Start your process and manage the momentum
- Motivate your mind daily
- Make clear and conscious choices for the energy you will surround yourself with
- Commit to the hard times
- Replenish your energy store with positive reflections of how far you have come
- Keep daily habits positive and productive
- Fulfil the promises you have made to yourself

My determination is the courageous effort I make each day so that I can continue to propel myself and others forward.

Power

Power is the ability to do good things for others

Brooke Astor

Consider that power is about position and possibility. In this way, it should be easy to envisage yourself as one of the most powerful people on the planet. For it seems feasible to recognise that your power as an educator is a force for good. Your power is also the meaningful way for making positive things happen in the lives of others. But the truest measure will be what you do with the power that is so precious. Will you use it to uplift, encourage, and inspire? Will it be your weapon for wiping out negativity, inequality, and injustice? Will it seek to right all wrongs? Whichever way you choose to use it, do so with the intent on having a tremendous impact on the lives of children and young people who now more so than ever before need you so desperately.

From this very moment, I will recognise the power I hold, and I commit to using it respectfully, responsibly, and responsively.

Decisions

You cannot make decisions based on fear and possibility of what might happen

Michelle Obama

In decision making-moments, we can often find ourselves stuck when trying to make choices about where we want to be and where we should be in our lives. These decisions determine our destiny and so we know the importance of getting it right! But at times it renders us helpless because the of fear we have that makes us question whether we are making good decisions. We must recognise that the more decisions we must make means the more options we can choose. As educators we know of the demands placed upon us to make tough decisions at critical times. But if our processes for making such decisions are based upon knowledge of ourselves, it becomes life changing and empowering. If we hold true to our moral code, our decisions will be based upon integrity and courage. This supports us in deciding whether we walk away or stay and fight. It reminds us of our power to choose to do the right thing in the right way because we can decide what, why and how.

In all times of fear, I will make decisions and stand firm in what I believe in; knowing that I have followed through on my moral obligations.

Flexibility

Stay committed to your decisions, but stay flexible in your approach

Tony Robbins

When will I learn that being flexible enables me to see a world full of possibilities? Where change is needed how can I maintain an open mind for fixing what needs to be mended? How good is flexibility for my soul knowing that I have options to choose what is good for me? In developing my teaching skills what more can I do to develop a flexible approach to imparting knowledge? Am I understanding that keeping flexible is my positive mindset? Can I remain flexible about my approach for creating success? How can I remain open to receive new things that will motivate me to welcome in new ideas? How can I make sure that adjusting my style does not diminish my authenticity? How can I see that being open to change will increase my productiveness? What must I do to calibrate the corners of my life that need realignment so that I can become a better example of myself?

I recognise and accept life's ambiguities and know that a flexible approach to dealing with it will eventually bring me peace.

Peace

There comes a point when you really have to spend time with yourself to know who you are

Bernice Johnson Reagon

I used to wake up at 4am each morning disturbed by the thoughts that I just was not good enough. I kept creating stories in my mind that told me I was less than my good self. I often felt diminished. I often felt troubled. My heart was heavy, and my mind was never at ease. Until one day my soul cried out and awakened me to the destruction, I was creating within myself. I had to make clear and conscious choices to eradicate toxic thoughts to create a positive way forward. And in doing so, I learnt that sometimes the greatest struggles are the ones we visualise within ourselves. By diminishing our power and worthiness we subliminally invite negative thoughts into our hearts.

By spending time with myself I realised that I had to reconnect with the harmonious rhythms of my heart. By gaining freedom from negative self-talk, I was able to retrain my mind so that it became my best friend. I realise now that my peace of mind is my armoured protection from confrontation, and strife. I let all stress go, no longer dramatising my life, no longer beating myself up. I let go of all struggles and accept myself as a beautiful person with amazing gifts to give to the world. I recognise how instrumental I am and the value I have in other people's lives.

Because I choose peace, I now laugh and smile more and shine a little brighter.

Sacrifice

You can never cross the ocean unless you lose sight of the shore

Anonymous

We are so thankful for your sacrifice in which you:

Limited your dreams for the sake of others

Endured pain to comfort those you love

Selflessly suffered anguish so that others could achieve

Stood in the gap; always making your powerful presence known

Never gave up on your commitment to support your children

Never compromised your values even if it limited your career progression

Made a difference by changing the narrative for those who needed you most

Always believed the impossible was possible

Inspired others by given so much of your time

Maintained your dignity when others around you were losing theirs

We know the sacrifices you make; never losing sight of the end goal.

Being human

In all circumstances, I am doing the best I can!

Ogugua-Gee Okolo-Angus

Considering all that I have experienced, I am simply doing the best I can. I am committing to my life work and not giving up. I know my flaws and am working to keep them in check but not let them define me. I do not have all of the answers and I do not pretend to either. I am coping with all that is thrown at me because I am doing things in the best way I know. I am learning more about myself each day especially my strengths which reminds me of the endless possibilities before me. I am being kind to myself because I know this is good for my soul. I am encouraged to reach for the stars at the pace I can manage. I begin where I am and with what I have and just work with it. I place no expectations on others for my happiness. I encourage myself daily and this supports my growth. I use my imagination to create an image in which my world knows nothing but peace, harmony, and prosperity. I commit to being human as I am my very own work in progress!

I am doing what I can in the best way I know!

Conscious Acts

Conscious Acts are poignant and pragmatic practices that enables our hearts and minds to be in alignment as we carry out our purpose. These acts resonate within our consciousness so that we may consider the possibilities for uplifting and motivating ourselves. As such, they support us in committing to a vision in which to be awakened to all that we want to experience in our lives.

Conscious Acts provide the gateway in which we can push past any doubt, fear, negativity, obstacle, or challenge and take steps for creating the conditions we desire for ourselves. As we step into our passion, power, and purpose we can put a declaration behind our intentions to open our minds and hearts by giving ourselves permission to bring only goodness into our lives.

Conscious Acts provide the opportunities for actively taking responsibility for the conscious choices and decisions we can make. And in so doing, we can accept and acknowledge unknown situations without holding onto any detrimental thoughts. Such strategies provide opportunities for us to proclaim our greatness by knowing our purpose in the world.

Conscious Acts fill our hearts and minds with the warmth of purposeful thoughts and actions for us to navigate the circumstances of life. In this way, we are actively tapping into our power and using it to guide us into a way of being that elevates our life; knowing what we are doing is for our greater good.

Conscious Acts

This section of the book provides you with adaptable examples of Conscious Acts you can carry out whenever you have the desire, need, or want.

In order to get the best out of this part of the book it is recommended (but not obligatory) that you:

1. Start with a reminder that not every challenge comes to disrupt your life
2. Start where you are, no expectations for what you might receive whilst carrying out each Conscious Act
3. Stop anytime you wish and re-start whenever you can
4. Repeat as often as you desire changing each aspect to suit your circumstance
5. Recognise how you are feeling through the process and make a note of this in whatever way suits you best
6. Open your mind to the possibility that the Conscious Acts can serve you well and be good for you

Becoming aware of the power of Conscious Thoughts

1. Become aware of all that you are thinking in any situation you wish to explore. Make no judgements. Simply become attuned with what you are receiving. Think of them as messages.
2. Decide on the best way to record or remember these messages or thoughts. Record them and review these whenever you wish.
3. Observe and determine which way the see-saw moves as these thoughts or messages emerge

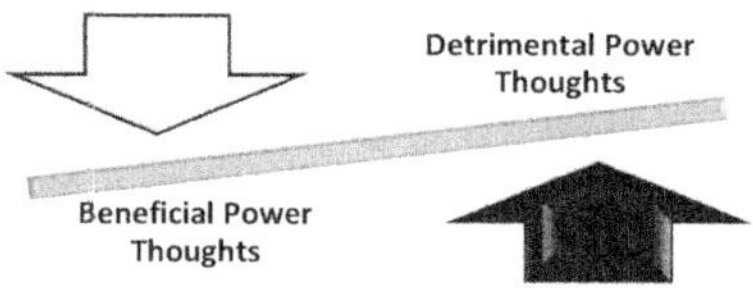

4. Determine if any patterns arise i.e., if there more beneficial or detrimental thoughts coming up
5. Set an intention and commit to actively de-charging negative thoughts, recognising them as detrimental to positive thinking
6. Listen intently to your thoughts routinely and assess how it is making you feel.
7. Try completing this statement as often as you like: ''This thought is making me feel or experience'.........
8. Keep a record of your thoughts and over time commit to redressing the balance so that positive thoughts out way negative ones

When you do this routinely you acknowledge negative thoughts and become more aware of how to diminish them as they show up.

Conscious Acts

Making use of Power Thoughts

Step 1: Find a space where you can be alone- really alone!

Step 2: Make a conscious commitment to really listening to your inner thoughts

Step 3: Focus your thoughts on something you did that made you feel great

Step 4: Hold onto that feeling

Step 5: Say three to five words that describe your great feeling

Step 6: Hold onto those words

Step 7: Now dig deep and hear your positive thoughts

Step 8: Affirm how great you are simply by starting with

I am....

Step 9: Make a note of all the positive things you tell yourself

Step 10: Find the best ways to make use of these as daily reminders

Step 11: Find your best way for recording all the positive things you tell yourself

Step 12: Repeat the process as often as you desire and ask a loved one to support you if necessary!

In closing

Dear Conscious Reader

As I extend these concepts, ideas, and insights, I trust that you have reflected on the contents of this book. I hope that in some small way it has shaped your conscious thoughts positively. It is intended to provide you with unlimited possibilities to see yourself in yourself and for yourself. In making a conscious commitment to embrace the messages within this book, I am fuelled with the belief that you have been uplifted. The intention for each aspect of this book is to shine a light on encouraging messages you can give to yourself no matter what you are experiencing. It is believed that this book serves as a vehicle to better determine ways to train your mind to agree with your heart.

I anticipate that you have received these messages with purpose, and this has served you well. I trust you realise the power you hold for living your life with passion and purpose in your own significant way. When carrying out your Conscious Acts, I trust that you simply recognise these as forms of self-enquiry, uncovering your uniqueness.

As I close this book, I am reminding you that your greatness is the goodness that the world receives. The purpose of which is to turn the windows of our lives into mirrors!

Concordance

Notes

Printed in Great Britain
by Amazon

66222080R00078